CHRIS BREMER

with Timothy Simpson

Free from ANGER

How to Reduce Resentment and Annoyance for More Personal Power and Clarity

*You are too valuable to get angry
over and over again
about the same situations.*

Table of Contents

1: WELCOME! 4

2: WHAT AWAITS YOU HERE? 7

3. HOW YOU BENEFIT THE MOST FROM THIS BOOK 8

4. WHAT IS ANGER? 11

5. WHY REDUCE ANGER? 15

6. HOW ANGER IS CREATED: A-B-C THINKING...............................18

7. HOW TO PREVENT ANGER...23

   CONNECTING INTENTION AND ANTICIPATION 23

   RELAX YOURSELF WITH "MM" 27

   GET OUT OF FOREIGN ZONES OF INFLUENCE 29

   BEAUTIFUL: TIME AND AGAIN! "HITTING" 32

   THE POWER OF THE PLUS QUESTION...33

8. CALMING DOWN: DOWN FROM THE WALL.....................................39

   THE TECHNIQUE "WWW" – "Wait-Wonder-What to do?" 40

   THE THREE MAGICAL QUESTIONS WHEN ANGRY............................42

   WITH "AAA" COMING DOWN FROM THE WALL 45

9. HOW TO PUT THE NEW IDEAS INTO PRACTICE 50

   THE "NOTE METHOD" 51

   LEARNING PARTNER...52

   THE $1 METHOD 52

   WEEKLY REVIEW AND WEEKLY PREVIEW 54

   HABITS CALENDAR..54

   AND LIKE THIS IT CAN CONTINUE FOR YOU 55

10. MY PERSONAL ENCORE FOR YOU: 58

11. MORE QUOTES TO INSPIRE YOU..60

The Donkey

(translated by Timothy Simpson from the German poem *Der Esel*)

There stood in front of the gate of a house gate
a donkey with pointed ears,
chewing on a bundle of hay,
thoughtfully and peacefully.

Now came by and remained standing there
Two rude boys
Who, while immediately laughing,
Shouted hatefully sounding sayings.

Their only purpose being
to make the donkey angry.

Yet, this highly experienced old being
Turned around in half circle,
Kept his calm and promptly showed
The side where his weapon was.

Wilhelm Busch

1: WELCOME!

It would be stupid to get angry about the outside world.
It does not care.

Marc Aurel

I will never forget that one particular day. I had led a seminar in Soest and it went very well, but I wasn't at all happy with it. In fact, I was really frustrated and upset.

On the way home, I wanted to buy a little something to eat. A young man entered the supermarket with me, obviously blind or at least severely visually impaired. He went to the counter to ask for help so he could find everything he needed in the store.

Maybe you've noticed that when shopping in the supermarket you often encounter the same people over and over again, in the produce area, in front of the dairy section, at the meat counter and also in the candy aisle.

I saw the blind man and the grocery clerk, who was helping him a few times while I was shopping, and I noticed they were having a lot of fun.

I thought, "Hey, that's crazy. Here I am, Christian, strong, seeing, enjoying good health, and in a terrible mood, while this blind man is in a damn good mood!"

Fortunately, the two stood behind me at the cash register so I turned around and said: "Hello. May I ask you something?"

He replied, "Yeah, sure. Fire away!"

Me, "How do you do that? How do you manage to be blind and to be in such a good mood?"

He laughed a bit and answered, "I can tell you exactly how I do it: How stupid would it be to be blind and in a bad mood?"

In every one of us abides a dream about how life should be.
Only life stands in the way.

Some things in life we just can't change and we get annoyed. Someone does something that gets on our nerves and we want to change it, but we can't. If we could change it, then we wouldn't be upset.

The constant theme of this book is to figure out how you can manage to cope when life is not going the way you'd like it to and when others don't do what you want. These are the cause of anger and frustration.

If we put that uncomfortable feeling of anger under a microscope it quickly becomes clear:

Anger is a storm that blows the candle out in our minds.

When angry, you are the horse, not the rider.

When angry, you're just a passenger and not the driver in the car of your life.

Anger is fatal to a happy and healthy life.

It's normal to get angry.
But do you really want to be normal?

I often think that anger reveals the true nature of most people and it is common to place the blame of our anger onto others.

99% of the people want to change others while only 1% are ready to change themselves. No wonder we have problems in the world.

So, be honest with yourself: If you are angry, who do you want to change? You or others?

3, 2, 1 – exactly! Others.

But against the will of others, you cannot change them. The "others" must agree and be ready to agree with your opinion. They must be ready to meet your expectations.

Where do your expectations come from? Your expectations are *thoughts*.

This is the first point to be repeatedly considered while you read this book. I like to say:

"*Try being angry without <u>thinking</u>. It doesn't work!*"

You are the source of your anger and not the others. In addition, the feeling of anger needs your unfulfilled expectations of how others should think and act.

If you are disappointed and angry it´s because your attitude is based on false expectations.

Think about it: how can you be angry without an unfulfilled expectation?

Do you also need stress, burnout, pressure, and time pressure as a prerequisite for your thinking?

Naturally, many questions surface when considering these things.

- Isn't it normal to have expectations?
- How can you reduce your expectations?
- Won't the possible solution quickly turn into passivity?
- How can one ensure that others fulfill our expectations?

...questions, questions, and even more questions...

After you have read this book in peace and reflected on it for yourself, many of these principles will become clear to you. You will become less angry and smile in many situations that are now exhausting.

We all have an idea of how we want to live. Surely, you also have an idea of how you want your life to be and probably among them is more sovereign serenity, less anger, less stress, and less frustration.

However, you also have habits and beliefs that keep you from this life. That's why I'm giving you a good opportunity to see through simple reflection what your habits and patterns of thinking are that keep you from living that dream life.

You are allowed to get upset. But you may also want to allow yourself to always be lowering your level of agitation.

2: WHAT AWAITS YOU HERE?

Of course, it is important that you first learn how the book is structured. Because the brain loves structure, and it gets it now in the form of a first overview.

- You will first understand why you are angry in situations without actually wanting to be angry.
- You'll also understand why you are personally annoyed by things while other people manage to stay cool.

When we understand such aspects, it is much easier for us to remain calm and confident. We humans have a mind that we can use to reflect and train to become annoyed less and less.

**We must learn to become better at knowing
the difference between reality
and our thoughts about reality.**

Maybe you have already seen that a picture frame can enhance a picture and strengthen its effect. The idea is to give you the frame first, place information about what anger is inside that frame, and discover that it can be a huge opportunity for you.

In the next part, you'll receive some wonderfully simple yet highly effective techniques to help you prevent anger. Then you will receive specific information from me on how to stop being angry.

Finally, I'll give you some really important tips, how to use this new way of thinking and the perspectives from this book constructively in your everyday life.

The only thing you need to do for a better life is to practice a few things that I suggest to you in this book.

The table is set, enjoy your meal!

3. HOW YOU BENEFIT THE MOST FROM THIS BOOK

Throughout the book I'll keep giving you concise, valuable, and proven clues that can help you stay calm and confident in situations where you're currently frustrated, angry or annoyed. I'll show you here in a practical and easy-to-understand way how you can stop trying "to teach cats how to bark" because that's exactly what we do when we are angry.

Of course, it is perfectly normal to get angry. But: Do you just want to be normal? Or would you rather manage to stay calm in situations that you're still upset about?

**If you want to get better with your anger,
then you have to get better.**

So that you can benefit optimally here and really bring your life to a new level, you should best heed these three points:

1. Your thoughts about reality aren't reality.
2. Don't just believe me! Try it out for yourself!
3. Keep it simple.

CONTINUOUS TRAINING OF NEW HABITS

Imagine the following: Your two hands are constantly slapping you in the face.

What would you do?

Would you just sit on your hands?

That would be one idea, but it has some disadvantages. Drinking and eating becomes very difficult. Driving a car will be eliminated if you are constantly sitting on your hands. You could also tie them up or even chop them off, but such a drastic permanent solution would be a bad way to remedy a temporary problem.

I think if your hands were constantly beating you in the face left and right then the best way to solve the problem would be to retrain your hands. Maybe first the left hand, then the right hand, and eventually both hands at the same time. This is what we are doing with your thoughts here in this book. We are retraining your thinking in stressful situations.

Remember: Be angry without thinking. That's impossible.

Thoughts about reality are not reality.

In a way, we think ourselves sick. It will be over and done with if you use some of the tips in this book. I promise!

CHOOSING INDIVIDUAL ASPECTS

The content here is based on 25 years of experience. But it's too much to try and apply 25 years of knowledge at once. I suggest you choose what you like and then try it for as long as you can.

The known is comfortable,
the unknown becomes comfortable.

There are always two types of truths: one's own and another's. What I am writing here are my own truths. I know that they help me and many other people, but they may be strange truths to you, after all they are my truths. By choosing one truth and trying it out, you can check and see if it can become your truth. This attitude is very valuable when it comes to taking your own path to sovereign serenity.

SIMPLE CAN BE EFFECTIVE

Now ask yourself: Can something so simple be effective? Can these banal changes and trite techniques really be effective? Yes, of course they can!

What you get here is not complicated.

But do not fall for two classical thinking traps:

> 1. I already know that!
> 2. Something so simple cannot work!

Both lead you to passivity rather than activity.

If you think you know everything you find here, I ask you:

Are you using all you know to end anger?

If you think the contents of the book are too simplistic, then I ask you:

**How well would you do
if you had to think about using 25 complicated steps
when situations become difficult?**

I didn't write this book to put beautiful well-sounding words on paper to get a big applause. Rather, my aspiration is to give you the opportunity to improve your life and stay relaxed when it matters most.

**The more complex the content,
the lower the chance that you'll use it.**

That's why everything here is not just written in simple words but also the content itself is simple. The only difficulty is the consistent application of the content. For that I also have some good tips and tricks for you!

Wait and see!

4. WHAT IS ANGER?

The frustrating thing about anger is
that you harm yourself without benefiting.

Kurt Tucholsky

Let's begin with the question: What is anger?
Here is my definition: anger is an unpleasant feeling of stress.

For me, being stressed is the opposite of being happy. When I get angry, I'm not happy. Therefore, anger, along with feelings such as anxiety, pressure, and being overwhelmed, all belong within a group of stress feelings.

There is a scale for anger that reminds me of some of the signs on the autobahns you see in Germany while you are in a construction zone. These signs have emojis drawn on a scale from "Rage" at the beginning of a construction zone, to "Feeling Good" at the end of it.

Here a 'Scale of Anger' from 'rage' to 'feeling good'. The goal is to be able to get to 'feeling good'.

1.   Rage: 😡
2.   Angry: 😠
3.   Upset: 😤
4.   Frustrated: 😫
5.   Irritated: ! [?]
6.   Annoyed: 😒
7.   Not so bad: 🙂
8.   It's over or feeling good: 😄

So, the Anger Scale goes from 1, "Rage" to 8, "Feeling good" as you go from the beginning of a construction zone to the end of it. The signs are valuable because it shows that it is "normal" to feel that way at each interval of the zone because everyone feels that way. It is showing you your normalness.

Anger, in my opinion, is always the result of an **unfulfilled expectation of others, life, or oneself.**

THE FIRST MESSAGE OF ANGER:

<u>IT'S TIME FOR A CHANGE!</u>

Anger is also a huge opportunity. Let us think about it for a moment. What characteristics do anger situations have in your life?

Does anger have the character of a <u>one-time</u> or a <u>recurring</u> situation? What do you think?

I think anger situations are mostly <u>recurrent</u> in character. We are always getting annoyed at the same things, people, and situations. In the case above, it is getting angry over construction zones! Your expectation is that there shouldn't be anything to slow down your travel on a highway. Least of all on a German Autobahn where you can go as fast as you want, and it actually makes sense to drive a Porsche, Ferrari, or a Corvette.

Anger is an opportunity and a quite positive one at that!

Unpleasant feelings are like voices speaking to you, telling you to learn new techniques so that you can remain calm, happy, controlled, and confident when you experience those same situations in the future.

Of course, you can continue living life like you have until now. Anger is not deadly. But if you want to lead a happier life then it makes a lot of sense to look at what your anger situations are, both in your private life and your professional life, and learn how to stay calm and controlled in those same situations that you repeatedly experience.

Unpleasant feelings make us unhappy in the moment we experience them. But they show us that we can learn new ways to be happier. Anger is telling us, "It's time to change! Learn to suffer less!"

Anger is now a valuable resource for new happiness, strange as it may sound.

After all, isn't the message of the pain from touching a hot stove screaming at us, **<u>"Don't do that again"</u>**?

It is not smart to override this message and ignore it.

Think about this point of view on anger:

**Our unpleasant feelings of stress, and therefore anger, are signs for us.
They happen for us, not against us.**

Stress and anger are telling us to pause and contemplate whether what we are doing and thinking is good for us at all. They are showing us that <u>it is time for a new decision</u>, to look at things from a new perspective, and to react in a new way.

Anger is always an invitation to change. The human being has a very ingenious way of functioning if we can understand what it is trying to tell us.

Our logic speaks to us through our emotions.

(We can learn to change our logic and thus change our emotions.)

THE SECOND MESSAGE Of ANGER:

<u>ANGER TELLS YOU THAT YOU ARE IN NEED OF SOMETHING!</u>

Anger shows you that to be happy you need something you don't have right now. But you can get it and take it. For example, someone who has authority over you has been rude to you. What do you need then? You need their respect. Your anger is telling you: You need kindness, but you are not getting it.

(You can maximize the chance of being treated with respect and kindness by addressing the issue to them as often as needed! Use the energy from your emotions to acquire the courage to express your needs to your superiors in the same tone as you wish to be treated.)

THE THIRD MESSAGE OF ANGER:

<u>USE YOUR ZONE OF INFLUENCE!</u> (Not theirs!)

There is another reason why anger has something positive. Consider whose zone of influence you are in when you get angry.

Assume for a moment that the driver in front of you is driving strangely. In whose sphere of influence is their driving style?

They are driving in their influence zone. You have no influence over them at all.
If your boss is treating you badly and does not lead you well, whose sphere of influence is your boss's leadership style? You are in his or her sphere of influence. You have no influence over them either.

As bad as the feeling of anger is, it is showing you that you are making yourself a victim. You are making yourself a passive person. Following the motto:

"If others behaved better, then I would be happy."

The problem is that they won't behave differently just for you.

(When you focus on your own zone of influence, how you drive, how you treat others, how you act in life, you are choosing to be your own person and cannot be swayed by the whims of others. The strength that is acquired through the acknowledgement that anger has taught you how to live on your own terms now makes you a person who naturally commands kindness and respect.)

Anger is an unpleasant and a nasty stressful emotion. It shows you that you have recurring situations in your life that make it difficult to be happy. So, learn to cope with it in a smoother, looser and more relaxed way by listening to the real messages anger is sending you.

The Three Messages of Anger are:

- **It is time for a change!**
- **You are in need of something!**
- **Use your zone of influence!**

The next time you feel angry, ask yourself which messages are being sent to you.

Of course, I'll show you throughout the book how you can translate all three messages in your life.

5. WHY REDUCE ANGER?

Now I've shown you what's good about being angry. However, as is well known…

> ***The dose makes the poison.***
> (*Sola dosis facit venenum.*)

> **Paracelsus**

The saying was made popular by Paracelsus, who was one of the first medical professors to recognize that physicians required a solid academic knowledge in the natural sciences, especially chemistry. It means that there is poison, anger in everything, but that it doesn't become lethal unless it reaches a high level of toxicity in a critical area of the body.

Therefore, despite the numerous "gifts" that anger brings with it, anger is still like poison and is always present and it is important to reduce it. That takes patience and a certain amount of effort. So that you can stay on the ball to reduce your anger levels you will need a certain amount of motivation. Just as you have not learned to walk, speak, or drive a car in one day, it will also require practice to learn how to manage anger. You need a strong "why?".

As you read this book, you may think, "Yes, I do!" - and then you will forget it after three days. But, when you have a clear "why", a reason you want to continue developing yourself and why you want to handle anger with more ease, you will have a much greater chance of applying what you are trying to do for yourself.

Therefore, I would like to show you some good reasons why it is really valuable to reduce anger. The techniques that I give you here in the book are simple and effective. Nevertheless, you must use them regularly if you want to benefit from them.

Why is it valuable to reduce anger?

REASON NUMBER 1: Anger doesn't make you <u>feel</u> good, it makes you <u>feel</u> bad.

Imagine viewing your life as if it is a parade passing in front of you because you realize that your life is nearing its end. Under what conditions can you say that you have lived as well as possible as often as possible? What has to have happened? What would your life have looked like? How red was your Ferrari? How long was your yacht? How elegant was the villa? Did you have bank accounts overflowing with assets?

These are all pleasant aspects and possible answers, but I think there is a better answer to this question. It is:

**"I lived as well as possible
as often as possible
when I felt as good as possible
as often as possible."**

It makes no sense to drive a Ferrari and always be afraid it will get a scratch on it. It makes no sense to own a yacht and feel seasick when you sail on it. It makes no sense to have a villa and live in fear that someone will break in and rob it. It makes no sense to have a full bank account and be constantly stressed about paying taxes. I believe that feeling good in life is the deciding factor.

There is nothing wrong or bad about having these things, but if they cause you stress, are they worth it? But, is it really those things that are causing your pain, or is it your reaction to them that is causing it?

Now comes the trick:

What kind of feeling is anger? Is anger a good feeling or a bad feeling?

When we get angry, we feel bad at the moment.
When we are angry, we are not creating a masterpiece out of our life,
but throwing more garbage into it.

Of course, anger is a chance, but it does not make sense to get angry over the same crap over and over again.

Just like a yacht can't make you seasick, it isn't the "things" that make you angry in life. Anger is caused by your habitual reaction to the same old things.

REASON NUMBER 2: Anger is bad for your health.

I want to tell you about three reputable studies that prove how dangerous anger is for your health. This is ultimately extremely important for a fulfilling life. If we risk our health, we also risk our fulfilled, happy life. Of course, you can be happy with illness, but I think it's better to be healthy, right?

Here are three studies from well-known sources about the relationship between anger and health:

1. **Stockholm University:** They have proven that people who are often and strongly angry have a _double risk_ of heart disease, including **death** from heart attack.

2. **Harvard University:** You have _five times_ the risk of heart attack for people who are often and very angry. For this they have been able to prove a triple high risk of cerebral infarction, a brain stroke. Just to make the meaning clear: that's 500% and 300%!

3. **University of Michigan:** There is a clear link between the susceptibility to stroke and the tendency to vent strong internal anger to the outside.

It is good to let the anger out, but to build up the anger beforehand is a health hazard and increases the risk of having a stroke.

I hope that these reasons are a good source for your personal "Why?" to permanently reduce anger and change a few things in your thinking and actions.

6. HOW ANGER IS CREATED: A-B-C THINKING

It's really fascinating: No one wants to get angry, and yet it happens to us again and again. It is as if we are spineless and can't control ourselves. It's important to:

- understand what I want to change.
- take responsibility for our feelings, including our anger.

In order to make both easier for you in the future, I would like to explain one of my most valuable concepts known as "A-B-C-thinking" to you.

- "A" stands for reality.
  - What *happens* in real life.
  - NDF: numbers, data, facts.

- "B" stands for your thoughts.
  - Your *thinking* about "A".
  - RIO: rating, interpreting, opinion.

- "C" stands for feelings.
  - Your *feeling* that results from your thoughts about reality.

EXAMPLES OF THE A-B-C THINKING AND THE SUBJECTIVE PERCEPTION OF ANGER

You probably know such situations:

- There is a conversation with four people.
  - One person says something about a sensitive topic.
  - One person snaps and flips out.
  - One person stays cool on the outside but burns inside.
  - One person says calmly that she sees it differently.

These reactions are lightning fast.

Nobody has to be angry.

This means that what *happens* in reality is not as crucial to your sense of anger as your *thinking*, your *expectations*, your *interpretation*, or your *opinion* of reality. If in *reality*, the

"A-level" alone, was responsible for our sense of anger, then all people would have to react in exactly the same way in every situation.

Most people can't direct their thinking.

Another example:

Imagine sitting in a sidewalk café in the summer
and a Ferrari drives up and parks.
A young man gets out.

What do you think?

1. Cool, he has certainly worked hard to be able to buy that car!
2. Well, has he earned that Ferrari in an honest way?

Then feelings emerge as a result of how you are thinking about what is happening in reality. Are you happy for him or do you have an aversion to him and are skeptical towards him?

There is always something real when you get angry but that's not as relevant to your emotional life as your thinking about the reality.

The truth about the reality above is that the Ferrari doesn't belong to the young man at all. He is simply delivering it from a repair shop to the owner who works in a building close by! Thoughts aren't real but they can really affect how you feel.
Think about the following sentence:

**"Without your reaction
reality has no power over you!"**

You can't decide in the morning not to think but you can direct your thinking.

Sometimes you have good days when you are not angry about something, but that same thing can really make you angry on any other day.

Please remember the following idea:

"Be angry without thinking - it will not work."

The point is repeated here again: Most people can't direct their thinking. We have to get better at distinguishing between reality and our thoughts about reality.

Our thoughts about reality don't have the same meaning as reality. "A-B-C thinking" is completely alien to people who are often and very angry.

People who suffer from anger make statements like, "I'm angry about him." or "Mr. Miller is to blame for my anger." In my opinion, that's false. If they were being truthful, the accurate thing to say would be, "My thoughts about Mr. Miller make me angry." I believe that when people get angry, it's because of their angry thoughts about a good and peaceful reality.

**Human freedom is the space
between reality and our feelings.**

As humans we have the power to choose between one thing and another. Choosing between having control over your thoughts and being a helpless victim to them is an important part of becoming a person who stands above their anger and thus creates a happier more powerful life.

REDUCE ANGER WITH THE POWER OF ACCURATE THINKING

Practicing these techniques is not so easy at first, but at the same time they can be like a springboard to immediately jump away from anger and into sovereign serenity.

The freedom we humans have lies in the space between reality and feeling. This space is our thoughts. At first, we as humans don't think of selecting our thoughts as a cause of how we feel.

Our brain, which produces our thoughts, has been influenced by our environment over the years and so our thoughts are actually learned, automatically conditioned responses. Above all, our ways of thinking have been actively and passively influenced by our parents, family and friends, education, school, religion, advertising, the media, and the accumulation of life experiences and formative emotional traumas.

It's _normal_ to get angry. When we observe anger throughout our lives at the ages of three, seven, twelve, thirty, and so on, we do not question whether it makes sense to feel angry or not because it is _normal_ to feel angry. We learn by observation and imitation. We learn that in certain situations it is considered _normal_ behavior to get angry.

<u>But, do you want to be normal?</u>
<u>Do you want to feel bad just because it is normal?</u>

TRAIN YOUR BRAIN!

Thoughts, which triggers our sense of anger, are created in our brain.

Motto:

"The Brain Generates Thoughts"

Ultimately, the brain constantly generates a constant stream of our thoughts. The brain and its workings have not been fully explored to this day, but there are a few intriguing numbers that I would like to give you to help you understand why it is sometimes difficult to direct your thinking.

When you are angry, you are the horse, not the rider. That's fatal!

A human being possesses one of the most powerful machines in the entire universe, the brain. Here is a description of the machine humans have to learn to manage. The human brain has...

- ...about **100 billion neurons**.
  - An unimaginable number, but it gets even crazier.
- ...over **100 trillion synapses**. That's crazy!
- ...circa **5.8 million kilometers** of neural pathways,
  - If we collapse and measure their length.
  - That's 145 times the circumference of the earth

If you counted the 100 trillion synapses and counted one second for each synapse, the count would take ***30 million years.***

In addition, the human brain processes information very, very fast. At MIT, Massachusetts Institute of Technology, neuroscientists have found that the brain can identify images seen in as little as 13 milliseconds. That is 0.013 of a second or about a 1300th of a second.

Let's try a speed test. "What are the last four digits of my cell phone number?"

How long did it take you to know that you didn't know the answer? Faster than an instant, right? Your brain just went through the entire memory banks inside your brain and came up with the answer much quicker than you read the question.

Our brain is infinitely complex and, in its construction and its functioning far beyond its own ability to imagine it. Because it is so complex and mostly automatic, we cannot possibly learn overnight to become its master and be able to stay calm in stressful situations. It takes time and practice.

**The solution is always
right between your ears.**

Relax and train your brain and thinking with the techniques in this book.

7. HOW TO PREVENT ANGER

In this chapter, you'll receive five simple, proven, and most importantly, effective ways to prevent anger. This makes sense especially when you feel anger, because the character of anger is rather recurring. There is no life without anger, but a life with less and less anger. These techniques will help you with this.

My job is to explain these techniques to you in a lively and comprehensible way. Your job is to pick several of them, find your own individual variation, and train until it becomes a habit for you until you can't imagine life without them.

Losers don't practice at all.
Winners practice until they don't make mistakes.
Champions practice until they can't not get it right.

Isn't it worth practicing to become a "Champion of Serenity"?   A life without anger is impossible. So, a life lived using techniques to reduce or prevent anger should be a welcomed skill to learn.

Imagine a world without anger. Wouldn't that be something incredible?

CONNECTING INTENTION AND ANTICIPATION

You have to find your way through
the little thoughts
that repeatedly
make you angry
to get to the great thoughts that
make you strong.

Dietrich Bonhoeffer

The first technique for anger *prevention* is the combination of *intention* and *anticipation*. I use them practically every day and am always surprised by how much it affects my day, although the effort is really low. At the beginning of your day, simply think about what your *intention* is and then *anticipate* when this intention could eventually encounter difficulties.

This is a way to set accurate expectations for your day, because you know that anger is created when your expectations aren't met. You know what to expect because you've experienced it before. These situations repeat themselves. You also know that the outside world isn't necessarily out to fulfill your expectations.

Let's assume that you are working on a project right now and somehow anger is repeatedly being felt. The connection of intention and anticipation then looks like this:

On the way to work you ask yourself, "What is my intention today?"

For example, you could choose:

> **"I want to be happy.**
> **I want to make the project relaxed and successful.**
> **No matter what happens today at work,**
> **I am and will remain calm."**

That's a statement you make on an emotional level. How do you want to feel? That's your _emotional intention_.

No one wants to feel upset, stressed, or angry. We all want to be relaxed, optimistic, content, or possibly even happy! On your way to work in the morning, take a little time to become aware of and to _clarify your intention._

Attention: This is not a to-do list.

It has nothing to do with completing tasks. The only question is, "How do I want to feel today?"

On the way home from work, you check your intention again to see how it went.

As an example, let's set the intention...

> "In a few minutes when I get home,
> it may be difficult for me because of the situation at school,
> but **I will remain a loving father.** "

Most people do not set an intention for their days, at home, at work, or in life.

Taking it one step further: You also want to check your intention.

- What obstacles could you encounter that might stand in the way of achieving your intention?
- Based on your past experiences, what could make it difficult for you today to feel calm and loving?

Because anger is recurring, it will be easy for you to spot situations in which your intentions may come under fire.

In order to react better, <u>anticipate</u> possible difficult situations with the following questions:

When will my intention today be in danger?
What am I going to do instead of getting angry?

That way, you have a good plan B and you'll smile when it's time to use it because you have accurately prophesied the future! Your expectation has been met and your anger avoided.

This way, you will have more control and feel less powerless. In other words: You become more powerful!

It's better to be prepared for anger
and not feel angry,
than it is to be unprepared for anger
and to feel angry.

It would be naive to think that you could define only one intention and believe that you can live it without resistance. Therefore, the combination of *intention and anticipation* is so important for this technique to work.

ANGER IS REPETITIOUS
THEREFORE, ANTICIPATION WORKS

Now here comes the tricky part! When are you at your wittiest? Exactly, after the conversation. Because it is then when you have all the good ideas about what you could have or should have said.

When are you more creative, smarter? When do you have the most contact with your life experience and inner wisdom: In anger situations or outside of anger situations? When is the quality of your thinking and behavior higher? When you are angry or before and after you're angry? Right, you are smarter and more creative before and after anger situations than you are during them.

**When we are angry,
our mind
is working
against us.**

Before and after anger situations we have contact to our life experience, to our inner wisdom, to our creativity, and also to our rhetoric. We can use this phenomenon as a preventative measure when it comes to anger.

This means that if, from experience, you are more likely to expect that you will come home and your children will tell you that they have done their homework, but you later find out that this is not the case, this is a foreseeable situation. Which people at work are more or less engaged in the project, you are also largely familiar with. The whole drama of traffic, which makes many people angry, is also absolutely predictable, because it looks like that every day on the streets.

You do not have to be clairvoyant to know when your intention could be in danger. Therefore, I urge you to briefly ask yourself once a day, what is your intention and when it could be in danger.

Use the three simple questions:

- "How do I want to feel today?" (Intention)
- "In which situations may this be difficult?" (Anticipation)
- "What can I do to prevent it, instead of getting angry?" (Prevention)

Here's an example:

I know many people who get angry in meetings because people are saying things that are simply not true and total nonsense. It's easy to prevent anger in this case. Just think about your _intention_ on the way to work about how you want to feel in the meeting today. You may want to feel calm and serene.

Anticipate by asking when your intention could be put in danger. Clearly, today in the meeting at 10:00. Then you ask yourself what it is you want to do, except to just getting angry. That's the deciding question with which you can apply the technique. You will come up with great ideas, such as first to be silent and then to ask a specific question.

You will find that you can come up with many good ideas that you wouldn't possibly have thought of if you had waited until the moment you became angry.

An ounce of prevention is worth a pound of cure.

Make the most of this first technique in the future.

RELAX YOURSELF WITH "MM"

Anger deceives the senses,
confuses the mind and clouds the purity of facts.

Peter Chrysologus (Bishop of Ravenna, Italy. 380-450 AD.)

Of course, there are many techniques for less anger and more serenity, but what now comes as a second method of preventing and reducing anger is a sensation that can prevent feelings of anger, annoyance, and frustration. I call it _**"MM - My Minute"**_.

"MM" is based on the following idea: The thoughts that you have when you are angry, are the source of your anger and not the behavior of others. For that reason, _"My Minute"_ is about calming your mind, the **"B" in A-B-C thinking**.

I invite you to practice the following three times a day for a week.

- Sit in a quiet, undisturbed place
- Set the timer of your smartphone to one minute and start it.
- Close your eyes.
- Feel your breathing for a minute
- Ask yourself these two questions:
  - "Am I still breathing?"
  - "How am I breathing?"
    - Is it slow or fast?
    - Is the air warm or cold?
    - Is the interchanging between inhalation and exhalation smooth?

Whenever your attention begins to drift away from breathing, return to it with the question, "How am I breathing?".

Of course, you can do this exercise for more than a minute, maybe three, five or ten minutes. Then you're doing "M3M" or even "M10M"! But start with a minute. Now you have lost the lame excuse, "I don't have time for that". The reason why this works so well is because "the less effort it takes to do, the greater the chance that you will regularly give your mind the opportunity to relax itself".

That's "MM". When you do this on a regular basis, not only does the relaxed focus on breathing become easier, but it also verifiably modifies your brain and mind to become more porous, to let thoughts pass by, and more open, allowing space for new ideas. This will allow you to stay cool in situations where you used to get upset. Annoyances will no longer bounce off of you, that would be strenuous resistance, they won't be stored inside you, that would make you blow up, but rather they pass through you and no longer affect you. You will be able to handle difficult situations with ease and you will be able to smile much more often.

Again, don't take my word for it. Just give it a try.

WHAT YOU SHOULD PAY ATTENTION TO WITH "MM".

When using "MM" there are some things that you should take to heart.

First, the timing. Repeat "MM" regularly but stay flexible. I know people from my seminars who have been doing "MM" three times a day for months and years. They do "MM" when they get up or after breakfast, sometimes while they drive to work or in the parking lot before they go in to work.

Every day before the first professional handshake, they practice "MM". They will use "MM" again at lunchtime, after work or before falling asleep.

Always planning to do things at the same time of day is unrealistic. Instead, it is better to set a basic period of time for practicing "MM".

For example, if you know that there will be a lot of stress when you get home, and you will probably get angry, then do "MM" before you open the door. You will discover and be fascinated by how much it positively changes your life.

I'm a big fan of "MM" because it is real and not "so" esoteric.

You don't need to believe in an eight-armed Indian deity of paradisiacal origin in order to practice "MM" and you don't need any incense sticks for it either. Nothing against all that, but the nice thing about "MM" is that anyone can practice it immediately without having to understand or believe in anything.

FATAL MISTAKEN BELIEFS ABOUT MEDITATION

Important: If you do "MM", do not fall under the very common misconception of "When I meditate, I'm not supposed to think of anything!". Nonsense. When you stop thinking, you are dead. The brain is an organ that constantly generates thoughts. If it doesn't, the brain is dead and you're dead, at least that's how most doctors see it.

So, it's quite normal that you sometimes think about your thoughts while practicing "MM" and realize instead of concentrating on your breath, your mind is thinking about a friend who is coming over later. Sometimes you will discover that your mind, your thoughts, travel to a problem that concerns you at the moment. Realize that this is quite normal and return to breathing with the question "How do I breathe?" Or "What do I feel while breathing?". This is the basis for calming your thinking with a minimum of effort.

Suppose you are at 80 with your average daily stress level (on an imaginary stress scale from 0 = totally relaxed to 100 = very stressed). When you get angry, you go from 80 upwards, for example, 10 points to 90. When you use "MM" you will lower your average stress level from 80,70, 60 down to possibly even 50. If you have an average stress level of just 50, when something annoys you and it goes up 10 points you are only at a stress level of 60, which is a lot better than 90! Make "MM" a habit. It's really minimum effort with an enormous effect.

GET OUT OF FOREIGN ZONES OF INFLUENCE

Who cannot endure adversity,
is not called to do great things.

From China

The third method: Think in terms of zones of influence!

We probably agree that you can use "MM" now if you want. The hurdle for this is so small that certainly the best motto for it would be: "Who wants to can".

What comes next needs more patience and more in-depth involvement from you at the beginning. Although the core idea of influence zones is plausible and easy to implement, it can be initially difficult for many people to adopt and accept them. This will require your maximum openness and willingness to see an aspect about life in a new way.

So, here's the idea: When you're angry, you're mentally outside of your influence zone. The thing that is making you angry isn't in an area of your life that you can directly influence. Consider whether you can easily change how other people drive, the way a colleague works, or the friendliness of a salesperson against their will?

The mental story of anger is, "If people would act the way I want them to, then I would be happy". The problem is that their behavior is in their zone of influence, not yours. Therefore, we are making ourselves and our well-being dependent on something outside of our control. This is fatal for your mental health and you are risking your emotional independence when it's based on the behavior of others.

You can't influence the behavior of other people directly and certainly not against their will. If you'd like to show off sometime with a technical term, "instructive interaction doesn't exist". Really think about whether you agree with the following idea: When we are angry, we look for a button to push on the other person so that they become exactly like we want them to be.

Here's the problem that leads to anger: This button does not exist in reality. By the way, that's a good thing, because if others had such a button, you would have one too. Then the others could push it and you would become the way the others would like you to be. What you can train is to first, catch yourself when you're angry and realize that you are outside of your influence zone, and secondly, that you guide yourself back into your zone of influence.

However, this technique works only when you accept the principle that these areas of influence exist, that you cannot change other people against their will, and you also don't need it. That gives you freedom!

THE INFLUENCE ZONE CHECK

How can you learn this? With a little patience.

When you come home in the evening, review your day by reflecting on when you were angry during the day. Mentally revisit the situation and ask yourself, "Which influence zone was the cause of my anger?"

You will notice that it was outside of your influence zone. In retrospect ask yourself, how you would have liked to react and what your zone of influence would have been. Personally, I use the two simple questions:

In that moment...

- **"...in whose sphere of influence was I in?"**
- **"...what could I have done?"**

With these two questions you don't actually change anything, because in the evening the incident is long gone. However, you change your point of view about the annoying situation and thus you will be less angry in a similar situation in the future. Remember: anger is recurrent!

Besides, you can train yourself to stay in your influence zone by retrospectively realizing that you had left it.

The key question for the prevention of anger is:

Do you concern yourself with what only you can influence?

It takes patience!
It is the bridge to get out of stress and anger
and in the direction towards sovereign serenity.

When you get better at catching yourself wrongfully placing expectations on others and focusing more on the area that you have control over, you'll have less anger. Train every evening to reflect upon your day. Always ask yourself in whose influence zone you were when you got angry, and what your influence zone should have been. This provides the necessary insight to make you emotionally independent from the behavior of others.

The Big Fat "BUT"

Often this perspective leaves behind a great big fat <u>"but?"</u>

- "But" I am affected by <u>other people's</u> crazy driving.
- "But" I have disadvantages <u>when my colleague</u> doesn't stick to agreements.
- "But" I deserve friendliness and service <u>from the salesperson</u>.

That's right, because in addition to the "<u>zone of influence</u>", there is a "<u>zone of interest</u>".

Naturally, you are interested in arriving healthy at your destination, to be able to rely on your colleague, and to be treated kindly. However, it remains that you still can't influence these aspects.
There is a specific focus question that helps me direct my thinking and my energy to my influence zone.

Right now, I want to be good at...

- accepting things that I can't change.
- taking care of things that I can do.

The <u>focus question</u> is:

<u>"Am I in mortal danger right now?"</u>

What the calming answer will be, should be very clear to you.

BEAUTIFUL: TIME AND AGAIN! "HITTING"

"HITTING": the fourth method of reducing anger.

Yes, you read that right, now it's about "Hitting".

Now that the *Influence Zone* needs some patience at the beginning, we can return to something that you can use to reduce anger now!

Hitting is meant for special days when an awful lot went wrong and you got angry much more than usual. Everyone has had such days.

The drive to work or to your first appointment was already unusually unnerving and then the colleagues at work seemed to have conspired together to provoke you. Not only that, the stupid computer crashed, and nobody seems to share your opinion on anything. In a hurry, you also spilled coffee on your desk so that on the way home, you were on the verge of howling with rage.

This is where the Hitting starts.

You come home after such a day and, if you don't live alone, ask your people at home if they are urgently in need of help. If so, please help them briefly and then do the hitting. If not, start hitting immediately:

Tell your family that you need a few minutes to yourself because you had a bad day. Then you take a pillow and go to a room where you can be alone and lock the door behind you. Close the curtains and now it's time: you hit the sofa, bed, or chair with the pillow for a full minute.

One minute. In boxing, a round is 3 minutes long. So, for this hitting exercise you are going for ⅓ of a round of boxing. That's not long, but short it won't seem.

I'm really serious and do that myself again and again. It's a blessing. It lets out all of your frustration. After violently hitting with a pillow for a minute, I can enjoy my evening in a much better state. I pointed out to you at the beginning that something banal can be very effective.

The first time, you will most likely feel silly. After all, it's very unusual for an adult to hit objects with a pillow. But if you keep going for a few seconds and the pillow really starts to swing, then you'll notice how well you're doing. You will notice that you enjoy it. You may get the impulse to laugh or scream. Go ahead and allow yourself to let go.

Anger is a feeling that gets locked and builds up in the body when the pressure isn't released. Take a look at the body language of people who often get angry over the smallest things. On days when you think, "Why did this happen to me?", remember the Motto, "Do not despair, hit a chair!"

Watch little children. They do this automatically. They sit in the sandbox, get angry that the shovel has been stolen from them and then they break something. They still have that naturalness to let out the feelings of anger, rage, and frustration. We adults, on the other hand, have learned to pull ourselves together. That's fine too. It makes us socially tolerable in many situations and is certainly also a professional way to behave. But when you start hitting a pillow against the mattress in the privacy of your own home, nobody's going to find out!

THE POWER OF THE PLUS QUESTION

If you expect great things of yourself
and demand little of others,

you'll keep resentment far away.

Confucius

Let's move on to the fifth and last method to prevent anger. In order to achieve the prevention of anger, it makes sense to reduce the number of situations in which anger is made possible.

It is important to address directly and clearly **_what_** makes us angry. This is very difficult for many but is of the utmost importance! Otherwise we have not done everything we can to reduce these situations.

At the beginning of the book you read about the idea that you can learn techniques to remain calm, confident and happy in situations that would normally make you angry. Maybe you can also learn to become better at identifying **_what_** gets on your nerves, **_what_** makes you angry, and **_what_** sends you into rage.

But the feeling tells you something else very important:

Anger is telling you
that you need something
you do not have
and that is why you feel so bad.

Are you following me here? If so, then I have something especially beautiful for you now. The questions are:

- When you are angry, are you aware of your unfulfilled needs or expectations?
- If so, do you address them?

Now, let's take a look at this important connection between need and anger.

- When you have a feeling of stress, such as hunger.
○ What do you need?
■ Exactly, something to eat.
- When you feel stressed because you are thirsty.
○ What do you need?
■ Exactly, something to drink.
- When you feel stressed because of time pressure?
○ What do you need then?

- **<u>No. not more time!</u>**

"Wait! What?", you are probably asking.

When time constraints are stressing you, you don't need more time. Instead you need...

- the courage to prioritize.
- the courage to work with a clear focus.

You can see from these examples that feelings of stress show that you need something you do not have or is an indicator of something you do not do.

- When your feeling of stress is anger...
- what do you need?
  - Exactly!
    - first a valve to release the pressure
    - then a way to express what you need.

I look at in terms of chances, which means they are like the odds of winning at gambling.

If I don't say what I need, the odds are low that I'll get it. But when I say what I need, the odds of getting it are much higher.

Please don't think in terms of guarantees. Because the only guarantee in life is death.

Life is more about possibilities.
Life is about creating opportunities for yourself.
Life is about arranging the game
so, the odds are in your favor.

Just be clear about the following idea <u>so that you can stop feeling angry</u>:

**The friendlier and clearer you address
what bothers you and what you need,
the greater the chance of getting it will be!**

Luckily, there is a technique that makes it possible to get a release valve as well as a way to address your needs at the same time.

It is known as the now famous **<u>"Plus Question"</u>**! (+?)

I will explain you its function and structure by example.

Peter is a project manager in a team with eight other people. Peter becomes angry at a certain person, because he often comes late and unprepared to meetings. He doesn't think this is good because it not only reduces the mood and productivity in the team, but also puts the project's success at risk.

Who does Peter usually talk to about it? Not in theory, what he should say, but in practice, what he really says. Does Peter usually directly tell the person who makes him angry, or the others? How is this usually handled in real life? How do you handle it? Most of the time it's not addressed directly to the person you're angry with. Even though we get angry at someone, we often don't have the courage to talk to the person directly about it.

The problem is that the other team members can't help Peter or the tardy team member. If Peter doesn't tell the person directly, clearly, and kindly what is making him angry, then he isn't maximizing the odds of getting what he needs in order to prevent him from getting angry in the future. Plus, the team member won't improve, the team becomes less productive, and the odds increase that the project will fail.

Anger shows you that you have a legitimate need and a legitimate expectation. It is your job and your opportunity to ensure that your needs and expectations have the greatest chance of being met.

Many are afraid to say what they mean and need. I believe that...

Life is too short, to play it safe.
You have to decide to take risks and be courageous and strong.

HOW TO USE THE PLUS QUESTION

Let's stay with the previous example with Peter and his team:

Now the plus question will be used. In private, Peter goes to the person and says in a friendly but very determined tone: "Good morning Mr. Team Member! This important project really needs your expertise in the field of IT to be a success. Is it possible for you to come on time in the future and prepare better?"

That was a "<u>plus question</u>", which consists of two phases. First, the person is addressed honestly and is concretely uplifted. He is told that he is important to the project and that his expertise is valued by him and the team. This is the + Plus phase. Secondly, the team member is kindly asked for what would soothe Peter's anger. This is the ? Question phase.

This increases the chance that Peter's expectations and needs, which can't be fulfilled when he is angry, will be fulfilled in the future.

In the example, Peter said in the first phase: "This important project needs your expertise in IT for its success." That's the plus phase in the plus question. Peter is valuing the person from the heart genuinely and authentically. Why? Because he is maximizing the odds of getting what he needs in the future.

In the second phase, Peter then again addresses his needs by asking the question using facts and information about what it is he needs in order to prevent himself of being angry in the future. In Peter's example, the question is: "Are you ready to come on time and prepare better in the future?"

Peter isn't screaming, "You lazy sack of dung! Get here on time! Who do you think you are?" or snap accusingly "How can you possibly always come late and let us all down?!"

In the example Peter is asking directly, friendly, and honestly, for what he needs.

THE PSYCHOLOGICAL BACKGROUND

Now it's time for some important psychology.

Even if you don't feel like it,

don't say <u>what</u> is making you angry,
say <u>what you need</u> in order for you to stop getting angry.

This is a small but subtle difference with immense positive effect on the chance to get what you need.

Here's my life experience, maybe you can share it and then use the plus question more often in the future:
If I tell the person what is making me angry, it's quickly perceived as an accusation or an attack. This reduces the chance of getting what I need. By contrast, when I maximize

the opportunity to get what I need by asking for it in a friendly and respectful tonality, it becomes much more acceptable and opens the person I am speaking to which leads to a real conversation, rather than have that person close themselves towards me because of my judgmental tone, ending all possibility for a constructive discussion, and prevents me from getting what I need.

For the best results, I also pay attention to the following criteria: I speak

- very clearly
- very distinctly
- very calmly
- very slowly
- with a fixed eye contact
- and preferably in private.

Of course, the person does not have to fulfill what I want, but I maximize the odds of getting what I need. I maximize the ability to meet my expectations. I maximize the odds of not getting angry.

Most of all, I am improving the odds that I will always feel good in the future.

By the way, expectation comes from waiting. You can wait a long time to fulfill your expectations, if you don't do everything in your power to get it fulfilled.

Why wait? You can possibly get what you need now, and have your expectations fulfilled sooner when you start implementing this technique in your daily life.

This is the plus question.

8. CALMING DOWN: DOWN FROM THE WALL

Speak when you are angry
and you will be giving the best speech
you will ever regret.

Ambrose Bierce

Now that you have received five simple and effective methods to prevent anger in the last chapters, it is time to explore the "King's Discipline" or the most challenging discipline: "Come Down from the Palm Tree", or "Come Down from the Wall"!

Basically, it means: **_"Get over it!"_**

For this you will receive three different methods as we move forward. These are purposefully designed to have just a few steps. After all, it is hard to pay attention to even a few steps when we get angry. Or, can you remember 18 steps when you're angry? Hardly, because anger blows out the candle of the mind. Anger makes you stupid. Training with these few methods will help you come down from the wall.

From now on, consider all unnerving situations as welcomed training situations.

Of course, you may choose to use only one step of the method or create a personal mix from all three!

After all, you know better than anyone what will work best for you.

THE ANGER CURVE

How do we manage to get driven up a wall? Even though we know that it doesn't do any good for us and is a complete waste of energy, we do it completely automatically, as if we were on autopilot.

Therefore, this method won't help you to never get upset again. That won't ever happen because there is no such thing as life without anger. But they will help keep you from getting angry as often and stop you from being driven up the wall quite so high.
You can imagine it like a curved graph line that runs from bottom left to top right. At the beginning, the lightning strikes nearby, the thunder claps, and it scares you to death sending you up the wall. This is a spontaneous and normal reaction to a stimulus. In life it may happen for example when someone says, "You should have known that!" When

you hear this you spontaneously and without thinking are automatically sent up the wall again. This is also an immediate and unconscious reflex to a stimulus. The art to this method is not to come down off the wall within a short period of time because while it is a common misconception this is not possible.

The art of the method is to first realize that you have been driven up the wall and then find a way to calm down a bit. It is impossible and not necessary to go from 100 to 0 on the scale from anger to serenity. When you're at 100, a state of complete anger; your thinking, feeling, and speaking is far too destructive and negative. But if you are at 70, 80 or even 90, then it is already more constructive and positive than at 100.

You already know the phrases "Blind with Anger" and "Anger Makes You Stupid" from reading the first part of my book.

We weren't built with a magical button to press where you can turn anger on and off. It doesn't exist and you don't need it either. After all, anger won't kill you. It's enough to first _realize_ that you are angry and then _decide_ to come down slowly from the wall. This is possible for humans because of the ability to be aware, to reason, and to reflect on what is happening to us. Let's get to the first technique.

THE TECHNIQUE "WWW" – "Wait-Wonder-What to do?"

I love shortcuts because they help remind us of the plan we made, while we were in a peaceful state, to be applied during stressful moments in real life situations. They also give us a solid anchor to orient our thoughts, so that we can begin to come up with better, new thoughts during real life situations of anger.

The first "W" stands for waiting, even if that's difficult. The next time you get angry, don't do anything for a moment. WAIT! Practice it until you can. The motto is:

When I get angry, I wait.
I don't do anything at first.

Keep breathing in and out and maybe do a little "SMTO" (smile more than others) and grin a bit for yourself! Not as if you were about to go crazy, but a very mild, barely visible to others grinning is enough. Wait a while, you could possibly look into the distance or think of something nice but require yourself to wait a bit first.

The good news is that we humans can't really stay angry over anything longer than a few seconds. We naturally calm down by ourselves. Treat yourself to this room of time and wait a moment without saying anything.

I give myself the command, "Christian, shut up for a moment!" I realize that I'm in a disturbed mental state and I'd probably say something I'd be sorry for as a result. It would only cause more anger and make the situation even worse for me and everybody else.

Therefore: Whenever you feel angry from now on, train yourself with this motto:

When I get angry,
I don't do anything at first.

The second "W" stands for "Wonder", in the sense of a miracle! The background is that anger always needs a rating. We must evaluate others or ourselves if we want to get angry at others or ourselves. To wonder is exactly the opposite of evaluate.

For example, let's say you get mad at your boss. You wait and then wonder, how "such a person" could become a boss. In real life you'll smile.

You come home and get angry at your child. You wait and wonder how this little dwarf has yet to understand how to act like adults want them to act.

There, too, you'll smile again!

The character of wondering is one of amazement and observation.

> "Wow, isn't it amazing that my kid went out and
> jumped up and down in mud puddles,
> tracked it throughout the house and
> just looks at me laughing his head off?"

If you have some time and want to dig deeper into the psychological knowledge about anger, then you'll quickly find that it's always about neither repressing the emotion nor to blindly pursue it. The idea is to distance oneself from the feeling and not be controlled and carried away by it. Wondering helps you because it is more about <u>observation</u> than <u>evaluation</u>. From this "Bird's Eye View" you gain a certain distance to what is happening right now. Gentle humor is a big help in this step.

The third "W" stands for the question: **What**? What can I do now?

You have already read that when you are angry the idea is to get out of the <u>other's influence zone</u> into <u>your own influence zone.</u>

That's exactly what you can do with this question. Remember: serenity is not passivity. It is an emotional state in which you can act in a sovereign and purposeful way. Only with action can we positively influence our lives.

TRAIN "WWW" STEP BY STEP

The Point is: in the future, consider all the people and situations that anger you as welcome training partners. Remember the motto:

"How nice dear boss, dear car driver, dear colleague, dear husband, that I can now practice on you!"

**Which person that annoys you today,
do you want to welcome
as your future sparring partner?**

Please do not let anyone tell you that you can heed more than three things in anger situations. You may have heard that anger is like a storm blowing the candle out in the mind. Three things may already be too much. Begin with waiting. Train for the first week or for the first month whenever you are angry or even slightly annoyed, to do nothing at first. Only then can you add on the "Wonder". If these two first steps work for you, then in a third step you will be able to ask yourself **what** you can do.

Please take your time and do not expect yourself to perfectly master these three steps. In theory maybe you can, but it's about being able to use them in real life and making them a new habit. It's not so easy when you are angry, so take your time and be patient with this technique and with yourself.

THE THREE MAGICAL QUESTIONS WHEN ANGRY

*Anybody can become angry –
that is easy;
but to be angry
with the right person,
and to the right degree,
and at the right time,*

and for the right purpose,
and in the right way –
that is not within everybody's power
and is not easy.

Aristotle

Now it's time for the second technique. Because people are different, you also get different ways to come down from the wall.

Remember this technique as **"The Three Magic Questions."**

Here they are!

"How is it?"
"How should it be?"
"What can I do now?".

THE APPLICATION OF THE THREE MAGICAL QUESTIONS

- You want to control yourself better when you're angry?
- You don't want your anger to seduce you into spontaneously responding to later regret it?
- You want to get out of the endless instant stimulus-response chain reaction mode?
- You know the "Bird's Eye View" is good for you when you are angry but have difficulty getting there?
- You want to observe the anger situation from a distance and think rationally about what to do?

Then these three questions are worth more than gold to you!

Simply give them a try!

Here's an example:

Let's say you come home and immediately notice that your children made something to eat but left the kitchen looking like a pigsty. Although you are annoyed you pull yourself together and say in an almost friendly tone,

"Hey kids, I think it's nice that you made something to eat, but me now having to renovate the kitchen, isn't good."

When this offer of peace is trampled on by a fresh comeback, it can quickly turn anger into rage.

Now it's time to apply the three questions instead of spontaneously threatening you kids with grounding, a ban on cell phone use, or withholding their allowance. Such measures should be thought about in order to be effective, or not?

Ask yourself first: **"How is it now?"**

The answer might be, "I'm angry, frustrated and annoyed. My children are so disrespectful. I would like to severely punish them. I don't know how to handle my frustration!"

Take the time to be aware of how you are feeling. Maybe it would be best to leave the situation by saying, "I'll be right back, then we'll talk about it!"

Next, ask yourself, **"How should it be?"**

Maybe you come up with the following answers:

- How should it be?
  - It should be harmonious and peaceful at home.
  - Everyone should contribute to a good togetherness in their best way possible.
  - Above all, everyone should stick to the rules and clean up their own mess.

The question that guides you into your influence zone is **"What can I do now?"**

You probably would get similar answers like these:
- I guess, I have to explain to them again about how they are to leave the kitchen when they are finished and why it's important that everyone follows a few rules.
- I should do that in a calm, understanding and friendliest tone as may be, so that I can reach them as well as possible.
- Besides, I should probably calmly show them the consequences of their actions when they don't abide by the rules.

Can you imagine that the result of these three questions will get you closer to your desired outcome than screaming with uncontrolled anger at your children? I hope so.

A BEAUTIFUL SHORTENED VARIATION "YES ..., AND ..."

These three questions are already simple and easy to remember. But I have found yet another shortcut with the *"Yes ..., and ..."* thought pattern.

Using the example above, you could have an inner dialogue that sounds something like this:

- "Yes, that annoys me now."
- "Yes, it's not right."
- "Yes, we have talked about it 15,000 times!"
- "I'll go now and talk very clearly and as friendly as possible with the children again."
- "In addition to the consequences of repeatedly ignoring the rules, I also tell them why it is important to be able to rely on each other."

This variation is valuable because you first give yourself room to be angry. You allow yourself to have the unpleasant sensations of anger, frustration, or rage during the "Yes-Phase". Then you use the "comma" and you say to yourself: "... and I'll now do the following."

We humans can do things, even though we don't feel like it.

For example, I can call a customer, although I do not want to. It works!

- I just need a bigger goal!
- I just need my dream of life.
- I just need the "How things should be" vision as my primary motivation.

You can achieve this by trying these techniques over and over again and using them consciously. Try them again and again. They are a great opportunity to learn to control yourself in times when you would otherwise be angry and shape your life to be as good as it should be.

Anger will never be completely gone, but you will learn to be better at handling it.

WITH "AAA" COMING DOWN FROM THE WALL

Do not worry that
Rose Bushes have thorns,
but rejoice about the thorn bush carrying roses.

From Arabia

Let's move on to the third technique!

So that you really have a spectrum of different possibilities to react in more constructive and solution-oriented ways, I'll give you another way of coming down from the wall. You'll then have several choices from all the variations to develop your own favorite method.

You have probably heard of the following poem to live with more serenity in everyday life:

The Serenity Prayer

God grant me the serenity to accept the things I cannot change,
the courage to change the things I can,
and the wisdom to know the difference.

Reinhold Niehbur

If you go searching for "clever sayings" that will bring you a more serene life, you will find many. The problem with such slogans is that although they are clever, somehow make sense, and most help somehow, they usually aren't practical in everyday life. They may answer the question, "How could I still see the situation?" but they don't tell you exactly what to do. They are more inspirational and less of an instruction manual.

I have worked on this in my own life for many years and will now give you what I think is the most valuable technique for being able to use the constructive and solution-oriented way of handling things that can't be changed.

It's a good way to be happy.
It's not the way I envisioned it to be,
but despite that, I'm happy.

Others would probably call this "enlightenment", but for me *this ability is simply an important goal of my personal development.*

For easy reference, this technique has three letters: "**AAA**". I'll always give you a motto for every step and, at the same time, a technique that's just right for you so that you can actually implement the motto in real life in a very concrete way.

THE FIRST "A": ACCEPT

The first "A" stands for the word "accept". To come down from the wall, there is an important prerequisite: **accept what is**.

Now think for a few moments about the following idea, because it is very important for the understanding of the technique: Anger needs a past.

You can only get angry over things that have already happened.

It makes sense to accept what has already happened because you cannot change it.

Now the tricky part: How do we manage to accept things that we cannot change? Relatively simple: With the question "Am I now in mortal danger?" Isn't that logical to you? If something doesn't put you in mortal danger, you can accept it, can't you? True to the motto: Better than being dead. You can accept the situation with the question "Am I in mortal danger?". The answer will always be "No!". That calms and relaxes at the same time.

THE SECOND "A": ANALYSE

The second "A" stands for "analyzing" or simply "observing". It is observing the situation you are in right now. This is the famous "Bird's Eye View" of which you have already read or heard several times.

Observation is the motto and the practical question is: **"What are my options?"**

For example, you get an email that annoys you. You can accept it in the first step because it does not put you in mortal danger. But naturally you are still annoyed, albeit a bit less, and then ask yourself what your options are.

- Option one: You answer immediately and shoot back aggressively with the answer "I'll get you back."
- Option two: You can leave the mail for a while first and then answer later.
- Option three: You can save the mail and reply to it tomorrow.

- Option four: You can call the person in ten minutes and then, having a clear head, simply ask them how the mail is meant exactly.

This is not primarily about finding the best option. It's about finding what the different options are at first. Because when we're angry, we usually see only one option and it is rarely constructive. In addition, we leave the passive-reactive mode and now correctly feel that we have control and influence.

With this question, you allow your mind to work for you again and you can utilize your creativity and your whole life experience. Anger makes us stupid after a certain level, because it gives us tunnel vision and does not allow us to consciously act with reason. This question removes that and leads you slowly into your zone of influence. It makes you aware that you have control. This is important because when you are angry you often feel powerless.

THE THIRD "A": ATTACK

The third "A" now stands for "attack". For that I give you the question:

"For which of my options do I decide upon now?"

Life isn't about making uncomfortable things seem better than they are. Life is about improving your conscious actions to actually make things better. That's what you achieve when you...

**...consciously decide on one of your options
and to consistently implement them.**

CHOOSE YOUR PERSONAL TECHNIQUE NOW

Find out by experimenting which of the three techniques is most valuable to you. You can also look at it as a tool kit. Simply take it from your "WWW" set of tools or your "AAA" set of tools, and choose whichever seems the most helpful, useful, and practicable. This is how you can create your own personal approach and strategy.

Remember, I can only make suggestions, after all, I do not know you. But you know yourself and know best how you tick. Whether you're doing "WAW" or "AWA" or some other combination, the main thing is to get up and go on the journey to serenity. Give them a try! You can't assume that once you've read the book you can immediately do everything you have read. Following this chapter, I'll give you a lot of tips so you can begin to train and practice what you have read.

9. HOW TO PUT THE NEW IDEAS INTO PRACTICE

It is impossible to give someone an offense,
if he does not want to take it.

Friedrich von Schlegel

Now that you've received many different perspectives and techniques that you can use to positively view anger, you will be able to prevent anger and calm yourself down.

Now, it's about helping you implement a selection from what you've read. Naturally, it requires a certain amount of effort because it's sometimes difficult to integrate new ways of doing things into your everyday life.

But I'll begin by giving you two important clues:

- First: "hard" and "impossible" are two different things.
- Second, when we are faced with deciding to do the "right thing" or "the easy thing", it's usually better to do the right thing.
- You can only master what you practice.

You can know everything about sovereign serenity
without being serene or sovereign.

Therefore, I think the attitude "I know everything already!" is a very dangerous phrase, because the question is actually: "Are you doing what you know?"

No one knows if you can do everything you set out to do, but one thing is certain:

"It's possible!"

That's the focus. And another extra energy:

"The 'known' is beautiful,
the 'unknown' will be beautiful."

I repeatedly observe that most people are working intensively at something, whether it is their career, their home, or their car. These people, of course, can continue to work on those things, but parallel to those external things, they can also start to work more on themselves and their inner world.

The bottom line is that you'll become more serene and less angry if you consistently use a small dose of this book. First you sow the seeds, then you harvest the crop. The reason being...

**"You do not get what you want in life,
you get what you deserve."**

If you are a person who doesn't care about serenity, who repeatedly gets mad about little things, then you deserve to get upset over little things. When you start using and trying out new perspectives and techniques, you will deserve to be more relaxed and you will actually be more relaxed. If your anger issues need to be improved, then you will have to get better.

If you cannot do something today it only means you will be able to do it tomorrow. For this you only need to try one technique or the other more often. For that, I'll give you some valuable tips.

**Nobody knows if you can do it.
But one thing is certain: it is possible!**

THE "NOTE METHOD"

The first tip is my note method. It is as simple as it is effective. You only have to follow my directions exactly and consistently if you want them to work for you.

To begin, pick one thing out of this book. Write this down on a piece of paper first thing in the morning and say to yourself: "This is my goal for today. I will pay attention to this." For example, write down that you'll do the <u>"Plus Question"</u> a few times or practice <u>"MM"</u> three times. Take another closer look at the note and put it in your pocket. If you think about it, look at it a few times throughout the day and heed what you wrote down.

When you come home in the evening, you look at it again and you may think, "Look! I didn't do that. How good is it that I realized that I didn't do it!" The chance that you don't do it is very big in the beginning. However, the note is responsible for making a very significant difference.

- If you set a goal, don't do it, and you realize that you have not done it, you have no problem.

- If you set a goal, don't do it, and you don't realize it you haven't done it, you have a problem.

That is the value behind the "Note Method". At some point you will be so annoyed that you write a new note every morning and every night only to realize that you have not done it, that you will then finally start doing it.

I like the note method and have been able to change my behavior and thinking several times in important ways. You just have to write notes until they are no longer necessary, because you have built a new habit with them. Get on your own nerves for as long as it takes!

LEARNING PARTNER

The second method: look for a learning partner. Many people want to try something and practice a new behavior and do it alone. That's a crazy idea! That's not necessary, after all, you'll probably have two or three good friends to go to and say, "Hey, I need your help. Can we call once a week for 10 minutes? I'll tell you on the phone what I've been up to over the past week and what I've done about it. Then I'll tell you what I'm doing for the next week. Would you mind helping me change a certain part of my behavior?"

You're sure to find someone who will gladly help you do something that's important to you. For example, if you complain on Wednesday about doing what you said you were going to do, but you know that you'll be asked on Monday, that's very helpful.

THE $1 METHOD

The third method is my $1 method and that is a bit more brutal, but therefore also the more effective. You can first use the note and learning partner method and see if they are enough to defeat the lazy dog inside you. If not, use this $1 method. It works well, as you will soon see.

STEP 1: WITHDRAW MONEY

First, you go to your bank and withdraw 100 or more Dollars in 1 Dollar bills.

STEP 2: DIVIDE MONEY

Then you carry the money to a colleague or home and then say to the person you trust:

"Ask me at the end of the day, if I've done what I said I was going to do for my project to become "more serene and less angry ". If I then say that I have not done it, $1 is taken and placed in another box. At the end of the month there is a sum of money from these $100 Dollars, which was created by my inaction. Inaction means, for example, not to have done "MM" or the "Plus Question", even though I said I would.

STEP 3: DONATE MONEY

Your trusted friend then donates that amount of money on your behalf to something that you do not like. The more pain you feel when thinking about that, the more it will help you become better. For example, I am a fan of Borussia Dortmund. Personally, I would have to donate this money to Schalke 04. The whole thing is a bit brutal, but it works.

We humans always want to be happy and don't feel pain. But what do you think motivates us more to new behavior? Towards joy or away from pain? Exactly, that's why donating to a cause that causes us really uncomfortable pain does help. It is painful, and therefore you will do what you said you would do to avoid the pain.

Where is the problem? You only have to do what you promised you wanted to do. That's possible. After all, you don't have to learn the Japanese language in 3 days, or be able to hold your breath for 90 minutes, or learn to fly.

**Learning works
through pain.**

I no longer believe in the idea of good intentions.

- When are the gyms the fullest?
- Yes, in January.
- In February you can train again without having to wait for the equipment.

I only chuckle when people tell me about their New Year's Resolutions, without coupling them with punishment when they do not keep to them.

Learning through pain works. This chance uses the $1 Dollar method.

WEEKLY REVIEW AND WEEKLY PREVIEW

The fourth method is the combination of a weekly review and a weekly preview. It is good but not as strong as the first three. I'll tell you about it because I often hear that the first three methods are "too hard" and that something milder is desired.

Gladly!

- Take time every Saturday or Sunday and review the past week.
- Ask yourself:
o   When was I doing well in terms of serenity?
o   When did I use certain techniques?
o   When could I have used certain techniques?

This is how you first reflect on what you have done in the past.

Now you ask yourself:
1.   What do I want to pay attention to in terms of serenity in the coming week?
2.   Wow am I going to take care of myself?
3.   What are my intentions?
4.   What problems could possibly arise?

This is a gentle and good method, because you stay on the ball longer.

HABITS CALENDAR

The fifth method of change is the habit calendar.

Here, you take one thing that you are going to do every day, for instance the Idea of "Intention and Anticipation" to prevent anger.

Let's assume it is the end of November. Print out a blank calendar for the month of December. There are many websites on the internet that will allow you to do this. Then each morning you think about your intention and anticipate the situations that may arise where you may get angry. You make a cross a day and do it all December and every day will have a cross on it because every day there will be situations that will challenge you.

In January you'll continue to do that but add a new habit to the list!

The advantage: that what you have learned in December, will already be easy, since it has become a habit. Habits are easy for us and the brain because they do not consume much energy. This means: in January you will be doing the old habit of intention/anticipation and now will be adding, for example, "MM". In February, you'll have two new habits that you keep and then can add a new, third one!

Then in February you will do "Intention/Anticipation", "My Minute", and add "AAA" and so on. In twelve months, you will build twelve new habits without much difficulty.

By the way, in my experience four or five habits will suffice to have a more sovereign composure in situations that make you angry now.

Imagine your current situation:

1. How far would your serenity be developed if you had started using the range of techniques described here a year ago?
2. How well developed would your composure be by now?
3. What would you already find easier to do, because you had already trained it?
4. What could you pay attention to now but still overlook when you are angry?

It's really great how much we can positively influence our lives by patiently building small habits.

For the transfer, I'll tell you:

Hard and impossible
are two different things.

AND LIKE THIS IT CAN CONTINUE FOR YOU

Smart people anger themselves over stupidities,
Wise people smile at them.

Curt Goetz

You have now gotten a lot of information, techniques, methods, strategies, and viewpoints. Now choose. See what suits you and your character. I can only give you information. I can't motivate you. You are responsible for you. Although simplicity is not always easy, it's worth it.

Let´s get in touch:
Christian: www.christian-bremer.de/en
Timothy: facebook.com/timothy.simpson.2000

Now, my wish for you is that you know that...

**...you are a <u>very valuable person</u>
and that you are allowed
to take very good care of yourself!**

Best regards!

Chris

10. MY PERSONAL ENCORE FOR YOU:

MY 5 BASIC MENTAL PRINCIPLES

I would like to give you my personal five basic mental principles, with which I manage to provide for my healthy performance.

****

1.   ***You were born to be happy.***

You were not born to be angry. It doesn't make sense. However, happiness doesn't often come all by itself, but anger surely does. Therefore, you will always have to do a couple of things so you can be happy.

****

2. *Your life, your responsibility.*

How often do I meet people who think they would be better off if everything would go the way they want it to? If only the others were different? You will never be happy because you give up the responsibility for your own happiness.

****

3. *It gets better when you get better.*

Others don't have to improve themselves. Leave others alone and see to it that you get better. Neither politics nor anyone else is responsible for improving your life. Only you can improve your life by getting better.

****

4. *You can, if you want it.*

Everything you have read here only needs your desire if you want to implement it. You don't need any special intelligence or talent for this. You do not need more than your irrepressible will. Anyone who has a dream of the next better version of themselves can achieve it by doing a little bit every day. It's easier than you think.

****

5. *It's easier than you think.*

Many people imagine the journey to greater lightheartedness to be difficult and strenuous. But that's just a mistake. You will notice that yourself when you disembark on it.

11. MORE QUOTES TO INSPIRE YOU

Be charming to your enemies. Nothing annoys them more.

Carl Orff

----

*Anger is like a storm, it isn't meant to be continuously raining;
it should clean the air and not destroy the crop.*

Ernst R. Hauschka

----

*It would be dumb to get angry at the world.
It doesn't care.*

Marcus Aurelius

People generally argue only because they can't discuss.

Gilbert Keith Chesterton

----

*Joy flees in all directions;
anger comes to gladly meet us.*

Wilhelm Busch

----

*Just you try and be really happy;
anger will come to you anyway.*

Wilhelm Busch

From today on, I will respect the following life wisdom.

*First, I no longer get angry over little things.
Second, everything that does not kill me is a little thing.*

Popular Saying

----

*When angry, count to four;
When very angry, swear.*

Mark Twain

Holding on to anger is like holding a glowing piece of coal
with the intention of throwing it at somebody
- the one who gets burned is yourself.

Buddha

How a person gets angry, that's how he is.

Arthur Schnitzler

We must also guard against giving offense to others,
and not let ourselves be seduced by it when someone else causes us a nuisance.

Anger deceives the senses,
confuses the mind,
and clouds the purity of knowledge.

Peter Chrysologus

It's in people's nature that they do not stumble over a mountain, but over an ant hill.

Lu Bu We

Holding on to anger is like drinking poison
and expecting
that others will die as a result.

Buddha

Anger does not help. It's useless, but it can destroy everything.

English Saying

Anger is a feeling that makes your mouth go faster than your mind.

English Saying

How about Chris Bremer (for Europe) or Timothy Simpson (for USA) as a guest speaker for your next conference or seminar event?

The topic "annoyance" is of great interest to many people, and their event lecture "Never again annoyed" is always rated at top marks.

Contact:

Email: info@christian-bremer.de

Internet: www.christian-bremer.de